SOFT TARGETS

ERRATUM SLIP: *Soft Targets* **by Simon Rae**

On page 38, the last ten lines of 'Taking Sides'
have disappeared. The poem should end:

But how did all this come to pass?
  Of course the Germans did their best
To raze our cities to the ground,
  But we've done all the rest –

A regimented school of thought,
  Committees filled with well-placed pals
To wave each concrete horror through,
  Tower blocks and burger malls.

And frankly, if the Prince of Wales
  Protests about this sad decline,
An awful lot of people think
  That's absolutely fine.

[9 September 1989]

Willie Rushton started his career as a political cartoonist. He had greatness thrust upon him in 1961 when he appeared with David Frost and Millicent Martin in *That Was The Week That Was*, and became an unlikely overnight success. Today he is still known to millions from his regular appearances in the popular comedy quiz show *I'm Sorry I Haven't a Clue*. He co-founded the magazine *Private Eye*, and still contributes a weekly cartoon (as he does for *The Independent* magazine).

His books include *Pigsticking: A Joy for Life* and *Superpig: A Gentleman's Guide to Everyday Survival*, both bestsellers. In 1984 his first novel *W.G. Grace's Last Case* was published to great critical acclaim, to be quickly followed by a new collection of his drawings, *Great Moments of History*, published by the Victoria & Albert Museum. Then came *Marylebone Against the World* (*The Alternative History of the MCC*), and *Spythatcher*, both for Pavilion.

His many stage, film and television appearances include Uncle Mort in Peter Tinniswood's *Tales from the Long Room*, Dr Watson to John Cleese's *Sherlock Holmes*, guest spots on *Through the Keyhole*, the *Kenny Everett Television Show* and on Thames Television's *Parky*, and parts in films such as *Those Magnificent Men in Their Flying Machines*. His recreations are listed in *Who's Who* as: losing weight, gaining weight, and parking. He is also a cricket fanatic, and is currently working on a musical called *Tallulah Who?* about Tallulah Bankhead with Suzi Quatro.

As the presenter of Radio 4's *Poetry Please!* and co-presenter of Radio 5's *Talking Poetry*, **Simon Rae** is known to thousands of listeners. He has published two anthologies, *The Faber Book of Drink, Drinkers and Drinking* (1991), and *The Orange Dove of Fiji: Poems for the World Wide Fund for Nature* (Hutchinson). He has won an Eric Gregory Award and a Southern Arts literature bursary for his poetry, and selections of his work have appeared in anthologies such as Faber's *Poetry Introduction 5* and *Seren Poets 2*. He is now working on a comic cricket novel.

That's the interesting stuff. The boring bits about him are that he did his degree at the University of Kent, survived briefly as a teacher at Banbury School, and then did postgraduate work on Clough (not Brian) and Arnold (Matthew) at Lincoln College, Oxford. He is a freelance writer and broadcaster, and commutes from Devizes in Wiltshire to the BBC in Bristol. He's also a cricket enthusiast – and a wily offspin bowler. He is continuing to work on his arm-ball.

Soft Targets

FROM THE *Weekend* Guardian

POEMS BY	ILLUSTRATED BY
SIMON RAE	**WILLIE RUSHTON**

FOREWORD BY RICHARD BOSTON

BLOODAXE BOOKS

Poems copyright © Simon Rae 1988, 1989, 1990, 1991
Drawings copyright © Willie Rushton 1991

ISBN: 1 85224 165 9

First published 1991 by
Bloodaxe Books Ltd,
P.O. Box 1SN,
Newcastle upon Tyne NE99 1SN.

Bloodaxe Books Ltd acknowledges
the financial assistance of Northern Arts.

Cover reproduction by V & H Reprographics, Newcastle upon Tyne.

Printed in Great Britain by
Bell & Bain Limited, Glasgow, Scotland.

For My Mother, Jill Rae,
Keeper of the Scrapbook

Acknowledgements

All the poems in this book were first published in *The Guardian*. The following poems have also appeared in anthologies and school books: 'Greatest Hits' in *Unauthorised Versions*, edited by Kenneth Baker (Faber); 'The Ballad of Hillsborough' in *Both Sides of the River: Merseyside in Poetry and Prose*, edited by Gladys Mary Coles (Headland), and in *Second Thoughts* (Collins Educational); and 'China Crisis' in *Agony Column* by David Curtis (Nelson).

Other poems have been reprinted elsewhere, and my thanks go to the editors of those publications for seeking my permission and, in most cases, for their courtesy in sending complimentary copies.

Contents

Author's Note

These poems were written for the *Weekend Guardian*, the Saturday *Guardian*'s tabloid supplement. They appear in chronological order – though not necessarily exactly as first printed – from December 1988 to the summer of 1991. How I first came to write occasional verse for the *Guardian* is told in Richard Boston's foreword, and it is to him I owe my first, very great, debt of gratitude.

Alan Rusbridger was the founder editor of the *Weekend Guardian*, and I would like to thank him for the risk he took in inviting me to become a regular contributor. Ian Mayes was his assistant, and subsequent editorial teams have been Ed Vulliamy with Chris McClean, and now Roger Alton, supported by Jocelyn Targett and Murray Armstrong. To them, and to Stuart Legge and all the others who have struggled with the eccentric typographical demands of verse, heartfelt thanks.

I owe a special debt to Wendy Cope whose telephone criticism in the hours leading up to my deadline has always been of the most practical kind. Those infelicities of style and tone that remain are entirely my responsibility.

I would also like to thank the many readers who have taken the trouble to write. Feedback, appreciative or otherwise, is always a welcome antidote to the writer's occupational isolation. My most regular correspondent is Harish Shah, of Haringay, London, and I am happy to take this opportunity to thank him for all the letters, cards, poems and personalised key-rings he has sent me since the beginning.

Finally, my thanks to Willie Rushton for agreeing to illustrate *Soft Targets*. I hope on some occasion to extend our partnership onto the cricket field.

Foreword

'I've acquired a poet,' I announced at breakfast.

'You've acquired a poet?' Lindsay said. Alan, who is a cool cucumber, didn't look up from reading the *Sun*.

'He's upstairs.'

'Upstairs?'

'He slept on the couch. I hope you don't mind. We tried not to make any noise coming in last night.'

'Do poets eat breakfast?'

'Rarely,' I said. 'This one would like a cup of tea. I'll take it up to him. He's working.'

'Working?'

'The sort of work poets do. He's got to finish by eleven o'clock so I think we'd better let him be. Poets like to struggle with the Muse on their own.'

'Haven't you got to write something by eleven yourself?' Alan asked, shifting his attention to the *Telegraph*. At that time he was not yet Features Editor of the *Guardian* – just getting in practice.

'Up to a point,' I said, and went upstairs with a mug of tea for the bard.

It was perfectly true that I was supposed to deliver a piece to the *Guardian* Arts page by eleven o'clock, or towards the end of the morning, otherwise known as after lunch at the very latest. It was to be about Vikram Seth, who the previous evening had given a reading from his novel in verse *The Golden Gate* at the Poetry Society.

After the reading a small group of us went to a nearby pub. After a while the small group thinned out to Simon Rae and me. One drink led to another. It was very jolly, so jolly that I came up with a really silly idea. If Vikram Seth could write a novel in verse, why didn't I write my review likewise? It was that stage of the evening when it is all to easy to fail to spot the most obvious flaws in one's own reasoning, the fly in this particular ointment being that I don't write verse. It was also that time of the evening when it's easy to lose track of time. Neither Simon nor I lives in London, but I was staying a few nights at the Rusbridgers'. Simon had intended returning to Oxfordshire. We gradually realised that if we were going to have another round – and why not? – the train from Paddington would leave without Rae.

Then I came up with another idea. Why didn't we forget the train, and then we could have another round and he could crash at the Rusbridgers'? I was sure they wouldn't mind. I don't know why I was so sure but I was. Then next morning he could give me a hand with my review in verse.

Came the dawn, with its terrible clarity. There was a pencil and paper by the bed and I got straight to work, as quietly as possible so as not to wake up Simon sleeping on the couch at the other end of the room. It was soon obvious that I wouldn't be able to do anything in the fiendishly difficult Pushkin verse form used by Vikram Seth. I would have to fall back on McGonagall:

> Yesterday evening I went to the Poetry Society in Earls Court Square
> And Vikram Seth, the author of *The Golden Gate* and other excellent
> poems, was there.

After half an hour, this (and further such drivel) was all I had come up with. At which point a slight noise at the other end of the room made me aware that Simon was awake. Not just awake but in the throes of composition. He had been writing away as quietly as possible so as not to wake me up.

'Let's hear yours,' he said, after Good Mornings had been exchanged.

'No, let's hear yours.'

Whether or not we tossed a coin I don't remember, but he read first.

> Dateline Earls Court: a poetry reading.
> A phrase to fill the heart with dread,
> Turn grown men into home-men, pleading
> Work, their wives, or simply bed.
> Should I be mentioned in despatches?
> I went along and here, in snatches,
> Is what befell when Vikram Seth
> Read from his book, *The Golden Gate*,
> (Seth rhymes with *Gate* it's worth your knowing)
> A novel in the Pushkin mode,
> (That's sonnets rather than the ode),
> Reviews of which were simply glowing.
> But was this quite stupendous feat
> Going to prove my kind of meat?

– he read. 'Now let's hear yours.'

'I'll go and get some tea,' I said.

Which I did, and continued to do throughout the morning. Well before lunchtime the thing was done.

The Golden Gate has thirteen chapters.
Seth started with the Contents page
– Each witty, rhyming heading apt as
Apt can be, but at that stage
I must admit to being worried.
The man was looking far from hurried.
Two hundred pages – maybe more?
We could be here till half-past four
a.m., and well and truly sated.
Definitely a bridge too far
For those of us who need the bar;
Worse, far worse, than being gated.
But Vikram is a clever man.
Not only can he rhyme and scan,

Depict the lives of star-crossed lovers
Around the San Francisco Bay
(And sell his thousands in hard covers
– A poet who can make it pay!),
As proved by every sparkling stanza
Of his superb extravaganza;
But he can also tell the time,
And, careful to avoid the crime
For which no poet is forgiven,
Seth signed off some time before
He'd choked the appetite for more.
Back to the bar. May I be shriven
For harbouring the slightest doubt.
This was a memorable night out.

Such were the circumstances in which, in April 1988, Simon Rae's
work first appeared in the *Guardian*.

In December of that year the *Weekend Guardian* was launched,
with Alan Rusbridger as founder-editor. Having seen the poet in
action at close quarters and coming up with the goods at very short
notice after a late night out, Alan evidently felt confident in ask-
ing him for verses of a topical nature. Simon's contributions to
the *Weekend Guardian* since then have been occasional poems only
in the sense that they have been occasioned by the news of the day.
In the other sense they have been anything but occasional. They
have appeared regularly, virtually every week since – about 50 poems
a year, and the high quality of the Vikram Seth review has been
maintained.

I don't think he has used the Pushkin stanza since, which is a
pity because he's so good at it. On the other hand he has worked
in a great variety of other forms, consistently and inventively match-
ing the subject to the right form, whether it is a pop song or a
nursery rhyme or Kipling or whatever.

It is often the fate of political cartoons that what makes you laugh out loud in today's paper is completely meaningless a few months later when we have forgotten what event of the day it was that prompted the comment, however witty it was. But the collections of the best of them (which is to say Osbert Lancaster, the inventor of the Pocket Cartoon) on the contrary extend the life of often trivial events and preserve them like flies in amber, while at the same time making an instant work of contemporary social, political and cultural history.

And so it is with *Soft Targets*, an ironic title which prompts me to make just one more point and then I'm done. Rae can be funny and he can be light, but when the occasion demands he can express grief, he can show a fine indignation and rich anger and he is not afraid of being controversial. They are not easy targets and they're not sitting targets. And he hits hard.

Reading them all together (as here) rather than one a week (as in the *Guardian*), they have a cumulative effect which conveys something I don't think is intended but which is extremely sympathetic. I get the feeling that when he is writing about what one might call a heavy subject he does so with gritted teeth. And what grits his teeth is that these heavy subjects force themselves on him and in doing so distract him from what deep down he feels is really important, namely the crack of leather on willow. Only sometimes does he indulge himself and actually write about cricket (and the one about Dr David Owen is a beauty), but we know all the time that our poet is not in shining armour but in white flannel and pads. He does not, thank goodness, push any party line or creed, political or otherwise. He has more worthwhile (if old-fashioned) standards, which are those of decency, compassion, fair play and of what is, and what is not, strictly cricket. And he's having a terrific innings. This collection brings us the highlights of the first century and a bit.

RICHARD BOSTON

Recessional (1988)

The junior minister referred to in the second line was Edwina Currie who was forced to resign over her outspoken remarks during the salmonella in eggs controversy. Other contemporary issues were cuts affecting naval shipyards and problems over extradition from the Irish Republic. Kipling, not for the last time, seemed the appropriate model.

The tumult and the shouting dies,
    A junior minister departs –
A fairly painless sacrifice
    Of someone not close to our hearts.
Lord God, a far more dreadful pain
    Is caused by cash chucked down the drain.

Unmanned, our navies melt away,
    Our shipyards face the final axe.
Lo, all our pomp of yesterday
    Comes down to cutting Income Tax.
Lord God of old, were we not told
    All good in life is based on gold?

If lesser breeds without the Law
    Refuse demands to extradite
The terrorists we so deplore,
    We have to show that we are right.
We'll loose wild tongues – and Douglas Hurd –
    Assured of Wapping's final word.

God of our Fathers, God of Power,
    And Lord of our Prime Minister,
Beneath whose awful Handbag cower
    The hounded men of Westminster –
Lord God of Polls, confirm that we
    Shall rule into Eternity.

[24 December 1988]

Here We Go Again

Joints are circulating freely,
   Girls get fresh on Rum and Coke;
Laughter louder by the minute
   Greets each really awful joke.
Someone's spiked the mineral water;
   Auld Lang Syne's a muffled croak.

Wincing in the dreadful half-light
   Of an average sort of dawn,
(Tingling hands grope throbbing foreheads),
   Frolickers are now forlorn.
Andrews, Enos, Disprin, Hedex
   From their packs are roughly torn.

Accusations are endemic:
   God in Heaven, save it, please.
Don't remember, do I? – Did I?
   That was just a friendly squeeze.
Wasn't me – you must mean Derek.
   What d'you mean, whose tights are these?

And so another party's buried,
   Another year goes down the drain.
New year starts the way the last did:
   Punctured liver, frazzled brain,
Guilt, anxiety and self-loathing –
   Jesus, here we go again.

[31 December 1988]

If –

The new year publication of state papers which revealed the Macmillan Government's cover-ups regarding the nuclear industry and the clandestine use of military force suggested certain continuities with the Mrs Thatcher's approach to accountability. Two notable members of her cabinet were Nicholas Ridley, who coined the expression NIMBY ('Not in my back yard') for those who protested against relaxing Green Belt regulations, while using his ministerial position to defend his own, and the unfortunate Paul Channon, Minister of Transport, who refused to let the Lockerbie air disaster interfere with his holiday plans.

If you can lie about contamination,
    From salmonella in the food supply
To wholesale (Windscale) leaks of radiation,
    Or Russian fallout pouring from the sky;
If you can cling on to the last few borders,
    And shout to History's *No* a stubborn *Yes*;
Assure the world you're clean while giving orders
    For dirty tricks done by the SAS:

If you can draw up plans to sell off water
    And lower safety standards for the sale;
If you can give our heritage no quarter,
    And auction listed buildings on the nail;
If you can come out publicly insisting
    That building on the Green Belt must make sense
Provided nothing spoils the views existing
    The other side of your own garden fence:

If you can seize a Triumph from Disaster,
    By turning up beside a victim's bed,
Then disappear on holiday much faster,
    Leaving others to clear up the dead;
If you can sell the world's best television
    To Rupert Murdoch's grasping myrmidons;
If you can promulgate an empty vision
    Of universities bereft of dons:

If you can quote St Francis of Assisi,
    While all around you fall about amazed,
You'll find the rest of it comes pretty easy
    Despite the fact your policies are crazed;
If you can make a cut for every minute,
    And justify your dogma to the end,
You'll wreck this Land, and everything that's in it;
    What's more, you'll be a Minister, my friend.

[7 January 1989]

Nursery Rhyme

The use in animal feeds of 'by-products' of other animals – heads, hooves, intestines, feet – led to the introduction of disease into the food-chain, most notably 'mad cow disease'.

Little Bo Peep has lost her sheep
And doesn't know where to find them

Their heads are off and in the trough
With their hoofs laid out beside them

Intestinal tracts are bagged in sacks
With the rest of the offal to bind them

While Farmer Jones has taken the bones
Off to his farm to grind them

Into the schlock he will feed his stock
With their tails falling off behind them.

[21 January 1989]

ASSORTED SHEEPMEAT PARTS

LAMB ITEMS FOR MAD COWS

SHEEP BITS FOR CHICKENS

Valley of the Dolls
(Slightly Satanic Verses)

The first public burnings of Salman Rushdie's novel *The Satanic Verses* –
amongst much else – coincided with news of a range of American 'prayer-
dolls' called Showers of Special Blessings, which could be made to 'kneel
devotedly [and] put their hands together, eyes looking upwards to heaven'.
There seemed to be further possibilities for the devotional toy market.

First, the Mullah doll; notice the eyes glowing with rage
    As he holds up a highly realistic burning page,
Saying: 'What do you mean, have we read the book?
    The author's clearly a blasphemous, atheistical crook.'

Then there's the Eric Gill doll (or Married Monk).
    This doll twists serenely at the trunk
So that the top half remains unaware of the scandals
    Perpetrated closer to the – very holy – sandals.

And over here, we have the Bishop Leonard
    Doll from the very lovely Runcie-house, The Synod,
Pronouncing anathema on the Woman Bishop dolls,
    Saying; 'God meant you for a bunch of molls.

You can't wear all this poncy regalia
    Without the divinely approved genitalia.'
(There's also a cut-price John Selwyn Gummer,
    Though Sales regard this one as a bit of a bummer.)

And by no means last, or least curious,
    There's the Jewish Orthodox doll which gets equally furious,
Saying: 'You throw stones or cause any kind of trouble
    And we'll reduce your homes to piles of unrecognisable rubble...'

Warning: Though always ready with a psalm or hymn
    These dolls are an anachronistic menace to life and limb.

[4 February 1989]

Greatest Hits

'Kill Rushdie says Cat Stevens' (newspaper headline). Shortly after the *fatwa* issued against Salman Rushdie by the Ayatollah, the pop singer Cat Stevens, now turned Moslem fundamentalist, gave his support for the death sentence.

Vile World

You know I've seen a lot of what the world can do
    And this is far worse than a bad review.
I never want to see you read, man; you'll be a dead man
    But if you want to run, take good care,
I hope you have a lot of nice police out there,
    But just remember there's a lot of bad – and Beware...

O Salman, Salman, it's a vile world,
    It's hard to get off without a trial, man.
O Salman, Salman, it's a vile world,
    You're being hounded for more than just your style, man.

Hard-headed Hitman

I'm looking for a hard-headed hitman,
    One who'll kill me for myself.
And if I find my hard-headed hitman;
    I won't need nobody else.
No no no.

I'm looking for a hard-headed hitman,
    One who'll take the cash and run.
And if I find myself a hard-headed hitman,
    I know the rest of my life will be done.
Yes yes yes.

I know a lot of fancy killers,
    People who can gun you to the floor.
They move so smooth, but have no answers
    Woaoooooah
When you ask, What d'you kill me for?

I'm looking for a hard-headed hitman,
    One who will shoot me through the head.
And if I find my hard-headed hitman,
    I'll spend the rest of my life being dead.

[25 March 1989]

Whispers

(after A.A. Milne)

The Pamella Bordes affair provided the tabloid press with a field-day —
'Commons Call Girl in 3-in-a-bed Shocker'; 'Snakes and Ladders with Sex
as the Prize' were typical headlines. It was reported that she had compromised a member of the government, and threatened a scandal on the same
scale as Christine Keeler, though this did not emerge.

An editor kneels at the foot of the bed:
    Now tell me again all the things that you said.
Hush! Hush! Whisper who dares!
    Pamella Bordes is selling her wares.

Is it a Scandal, or merely a shame
    That Pamella Bordes was playing that game?
She played it for money, she played it for perks;
    Quite frankly, she did it with any old jerks.

God bless Pamella, she'll see us right.
    Wasn't it great in the Newsroom tonight?
Pamella Bordes had no ID card,
    But getting a Commons pass wasn't that hard.

A minister took her out dancing, the sport,
    And now he's the toast of the great *Sunday Snort.*
If I open my fingers a little bit more
    I can see somebody's pants on the floor.

Is it a cabinet minister, or
    Is it that Libyan agent she saw?
We're certain our Pam enjoyed sex to excess,
    But did she have Semtex concealed up her dress?

She's political dynamite, and no mistake;
    The Government's just hit a nasty long snake.
The children are worried; and Nanny's quite mad:
    If I were you, I'd cover up quickly, my lad.

Get all your alibis right without fail.
    (Delivered by hand and not dropped in the mail.)
God bless the *People*, the *Star* and the *Sun*.
    O what have we done to deserve so much fun?

So, Lent's nearly over; it's Easter tomorrow,
    A time of repentance, heart-searching and sorrow.
Hush! Hush! Whisper who dares!
    The great and the good are now saying their prayers.

[25 March 1989]

The Ballad of Hillsborough

Liverpool's FA Cup semi-final against Nottingham Forest on 15 April 1989
turned into the worst sporting disaster in British history.

The Liverpool supporters
Were given the smaller end;
Crammed behind the goalmouth,
The fans were tightly penned –

Penned, penned in their thousands,
Penned in under the sky.
No one there had reckoned
That ninety-five would die.

The barriers all buckled,
They couldn't take the strain.
The cheers of jubilation
Turned into cries of pain.

And when at last they noticed,
The police unlocked the gate,
But the exit was too narrow,
And they'd opened it too late.

The nation watched in horror,
Stunned with disbelief,
As the shadows from the goalmouth
Stained a football pitch with grief.

An inquiry has been opened
To find out who's to blame,
But for those who lost their dear ones
Nothing will be the same.

For nothing brings the dead back,
Post-mortems, flowers, or prayers,
It's like reaching the top of the stairwell
And finding there are no stairs.

That drop into the darkness
Goes down and down and down;
And grief's black waters well there,
Inviting you to drown.

Never to see your loved ones,
Or hear them on the phone –
It's hard to believe when it happens
That you'll never walk alone.

But down at the Kop at Anfield,
The goalmouth shows it's true:
The scarves around the crossbar
Are knotted red and blue.

Despite divided loyalties,
Liverpool loves its own,
And every tribute there proclaims:
You'll never walk alone –

Not by the banks of the Mersey,
Nor down the terraced streets;
Beneath the great cathedrals
A city's warm heart beats.

And now in the cold spring sunset,
The Liver Bird's aflame.
The Phoenix rose from the ashes;
A city can do the same.

[22 April 1989]

State of the Tate

'Masterpieces in danger as Tate roof leaks' – headline. The Tate Gallery was reported to be in a perilous condition due to lack of proper government funding for maintenance of the building.

Matisse's masterpiece, 'The Snail'
Was missed by inches by a drip.
A fortune hangs from every nail,
   And yet the Tate's a tip.

The roof leaks and the buckets wait
Patiently to catch the rain;
The fabric's in an awful state
   The Trustees all complain.

Duchamp's erotic work, 'The Bride,
Etcetera', in sculpted glass,
Got baked and shattered far and wide.
   The thing's become a farce.

Replacements for it might include:
'The Minister with Absent Stare',
(Magritte), Modigliani's 'Nude
   Reclining on Thin Air',

A Rothko, 'Rhapsody in Rust',
Rodin's 'Curator with a Mop',
A still-life called 'A Pile of Dust',
   Hockney's 'The Bigger Plop'.

And finally, call for those bricks,
Julian Schnabel's fractured plates,
And Beuys's felt and fat to fix
   The gaps between the slates.

[6 May 1989]

Audenesque for Early Summer

Auden's 'May with its light behaving'
    Returns to me as I am shaving.
Outside the sky is blue.
    The lawn needs cutting and the weeds
Are taking hold where new-sown seeds
    Should now be poking through.

I hang the washing on the line,
    Assured it will continue fine
For hours – or days – ahead.
    The paper's full of cricket scores;
A distant tractor gently roars;
    A bee hums past my head.

Over the landscape, mile on mile,
    The rape unfolds its brilliant pile;
The birds are back on song.
    The beeches tremble into leaf,
Challenging the sour belief
    That anything is wrong.

But perfect worlds, as Auden knew,
    Are based on privileges few
Can ever hope to gain.
    Beyond the garden's uncut hedge
Millions teeter on the edge
    Of poverty and pain.

[20 May 1989]

Loxodonta Africana
(for Sue Roberts)

Although the Government came out in favour of a total ban on trade in new ivory, reports suggested that the DoE readily granted import licences to consignments of dubious legality.

Loxodonta africana
Browses through the wide savannah,
Noble, gentle, dignified.
Nodding heads from side to side,
Harmless beasts sway through the grass.
Poachers wait for them to pass.

Shoot the brute and hack its head;
Take the tusks and leave it dead.
Vultures settle, stain its hide;
Maggots multiply inside
Muddied meat behind the face
Lopped away in death's disgrace.

Ears flap gently in the breeze;
Innocent, kick-starting knees
Stiffen in the stench-filled heat.
Penises will not repeat
Reproduction's stiff command;
Man has made a last demand.

Poachers paid by weight and size
Earn a fortune from each prize.
Profits rise with each tusk sold;
Jewellers treat the stuff like gold,
Selling cuff-links, studs and brooches
While extinction fast approaches.

Crates of laundered ivory
Waiting for the DoE
Officers to tip the wink
Will inevitably shrink
Into trinkets from Hong Kong.
Going, going, for a song…

[27 May 1989]

31

BT: A Lover's Complaint

With thanks to Walter Harris, whose letter in another paper pointed to the perils and consequences of the new British Telecom itemised phone bills.

Who do we know in Rusbridge, dear,
    And why so many calls?
You'll have to speak to the children, dear;
    A bill like this appals.

    I love you, O my darling,
        But my pockets clank with change.
    The wife has grown suspicious,
        And my kids think jogging strange.

Why does the question trouble you, dear?
    And why are you struck dumb?
Well, leave it till after dinner, dear,
    The Tomlinsons have come.

    I love you, O my darling,
        But I've lost the dialling tone,
    And there are sixteen other chaps
        Queueing for the phone.

Lucinda denies all knowledge, dear,
    And Justin was in Spain.
The dog does not need walking, dear, –
    Not in the pouring rain.

    I love you, O my darling,
        And I'm sure I always will,
    But our love has been discovered
        Through that wretched BT bill.

[3 June 1989]

China Crisis

After a period of inactivity, the Chinese authorities finally sent the army
into Tiananmen Square, Beijing to crush the Democracy movement.

About a subjugated plain,
Among its desperate and slain,
The Ogre stalks with hands on hips,
While drivel gushes from his lips.
                                        W.H.AUDEN, August 1968

The Ogre's on the march again,
Displaying absolute disdain
    For what it crushes underfoot.
Tank tracks are meshed with blood and bone,
And Liberty is overthrown
    By soldiers who are primed to shoot.

'The People love the Army!' blare
The speakers round the People's square.
    The Army loves the People too.
In Avenues of Endless Peace
The beatings and the shootings cease
    Only when the dawn breaks through.

As Brecht sardonically declared,
A government must be prepared
    To de-select the populace
And then elect another lot
(A maxim savoured by Pol Pot),
    If that's what's needed to save face.

A figure tangos with the tanks,
And cyclists brave the lethal ranks
    Deployed to subjugate their city.
The random dead are triked away;
We watch the nightmare day by day,
    With outrage, impotence and pity.

Back home, Sir Geoffrey Howe's got tough.
He told their Chargé, that's enough;
    There's much at stake: the Royal Tour.
Meanwhile, Hong Kong should rest assured;
There's nothing wrong with the Accord,
    Signed, yes, in Nineteen Eighty-Four.

[10 June 1989]

B

The Rime of the Ancient Minister

*(for Simon Jenkins, who had exactly the same idea
only two weeks later – SUNDAY TIMES, 23 July 1989)*

Nicholas Ridley held a number of cabinet posts, and was closely associated
with the policy of privatisation. He was responsible for selling off the water
industry. An opinion poll showed that 79% of the population opposed this
privatisation, and doubts over the quality of the nation's water were further
raised by the discovery of green worms in London's water supply.

It is an Ancient Minister,
And he stoppeth one of three.
'By thy smoker's cough and glittering specs,
Now wherefore stopp'st thou me?

The Bricklayer's Arms are open wide,
I'm eager to get in.
The barman's polishing my glass,
May'st hear the merry din.'

He holds him with his skinny hand:
'There is a share flotation
By which the Government will flog
Water to the nation.

Water, water, everywhere,
And every drop for sale.'
The boozer looked at him aghast,
His features went quite pale.

'I once was very nearly sane,'
The Minister confessed,
'Until I came upon a sprite
All as a Woman dressed.

The Nightmare Life-in-Death was she,
Who thicks men's blood with cold.
"Ridley," she did croak at me,
"I want these assets sold."

And so, to cut the story short,
This frightful wheeze was sprung.
About my neck an albatross
Was very quickly slung.

"But Margaret," I said to her,
"The water's nine parts sludge,
The Water Boards all break the laws."
"Get on with it and fudge!

We'll break the rules, to send the fools
To their stock-brokers running.
Our share-owning democracy
Requires a deal of cunning."

And so I have to sell these shares;
Would you be interested?'
'Get out the way, you silly berk,
You ought to be arrested.

Just leave it out, thou grey-haired loon,
You must be round the bend.
We've bought a lot of shares off you,
But water – that's the end.

The stuff you're trying to sell us, mate,
Is not for humans fit.
It's even, so the papers say,
Got little worms in it.'

The Bricklayer's Arms were open wide,
And in the boozer tore,
Leaving the Ancient Minister
A spectre by the door.

[8 July 1989]

35

The Glorious Twelfth

The grouse season opened amid fears for protected birds of prey like the
golden eagle and red kite, under threat from the indiscriminate and illegal
use of poisons by gamekeepers.

There's a glorious tradition,
    When the twelfth of August comes,
That the landed upper classes,
    And all their moneyed chums,
Go out across the grouse moors
    With their double-barrelled guns.

And this is quite delightful,
    As their head-scarved wives agree:
The sky gone dark with grouses
    Is a pretty sight to see.
And when they've bagged a bagful,
    They all go home to tea.

But there's a nasty rumour –
    It's amazing what they say –
That to preserve the grouses,
    The owners gaily slay
Crows and other 'vermin',
    Like protected birds of prey.

Although this is illegal,
    The worst you get's a fine.
But when you come to poaching,
    With net or gun or line,
The story's rather different:
    Get caught and you will pine

For several weeks in prison –
    Assuming that you're not
Caught literally red-handed
    By some fiery chinless clot,
In which case you've good reason
    To anticipate being shot.

[12 August 1989]

36

View from the Box

Although England mounted a disastrous defence of the Ashes, losing to the Australians 4 Tests to nil, the *Test Match Special* commentary team remained in high spirits throughout, sustained by a succession of cakes and bottles of champagne.

Johners, Blowers, C.M-J,
The Boil and Fred, all Dear Old Things,
Muse about the state of play:
Allan Border's lot run rings
Around the hapless English team,
Playing as though they're in a dream.

Statistics mount with every ball,
Recorded by the Bearded Wonder.
The batsmen at the crease stand tall
And carry on their endless plunder:
Marsh and Taylor, Boon and Jones,
Border, Healy, Waugh and Hohns.

The sight of Alderman and Lawson
Keeps our batsmen on their toes.
The movement that they get is awesome:
Up the umpire's finger goes.
Pavilionwards the batsmen trudge,
But someone passes round the fudge.

Everything in sight's amusing.
A callisthenic clown like Hughes
Compensates for our side losing.
Buses form their distant queues;
A pigeon wings across the sky;
Morale inside the box is high.

Conviviality and cakes
Will see us through the darkest day.
Never mind the team's mistakes;
We face defeat the English way,
With banter, sticky sweets and quips
And icing sugar round our lips.

[2 September 1989]

Taking Sides

My Vision of Britain, by the Prince of Wales, initiated another round of controversy over English architecture and the right of a member of the Royal Family to express such strong views.

You may think what I write is crap;
    I'm sure a lot of people do.
But one thing in its favour is
    It does not mar the view.

And there's another thing to note:
    Another twenty lines of Rae
Does not mean twenty fewer lines
    Of Milton or John Gay.

But when it comes to architects
    The story's not the same at all.
We can't avoid the things they do,
    However large or small.

And in their making they destroy:
    Whole streets, indeed communities,
Succumb to cranes and scaffolding,
    And yellow JCBs.

Their concrete creed is brutalist:
    'Knock down the old, make way, make way!
This style is for the Common Man,
    And it is here to stay.'

But how did all this come to pass?
    Of course the Germans did their best

Dr Owen Playing Cricket

By the party conference season in 1989 the SDP had split from its Alliance partners, the Liberals, and was reduced to a tiny rump dominated by its leader, who spent part of the Sunday preceding the conference playing cricket.

Dr David Owen
Opened with himself –
There was really no one else;
The rest were on the shelf.

And like another doctor,
Renowned throughout the world,
He struck the ball a mighty blow:
Into the sky it curled.

Then Dr David Owen
Put off his gloves and pads
And confidently strolled into
The covers with the lads.

The ball soared high above him,
Then dropped, of course it did.
The captain of the team was calm,
He neither slipped nor slid.

So Dr David Owen
Caught Dr David Owen,
Bowled – you might have known it –
By Dr David Owen.

Back to the crease he sauntered,
And nobody would dare
To question his continuing:
He never turned a hair.

Eventually his colleagues
Escaped him one by one.
And all alone, in failing light,
He scored the winning run.

[30 September 1989]

The Hunting of the Snark: The Baker's Tale
(after Lewis Carroll)

It was a difficult time for the Tories too, with the first mutterings of dissent against Mrs Thatcher, a resurgence of Labour in the polls, and an increasingly difficult financial climate. Kenneth Baker, then Chairman, rallied the troops with a loyal and combative speech.

They roused him with muffins and potted shrimp rolls,
    They roused him with mustard and cress;
They roused him with jam and with fake Mori polls –
    They set him exchange rates to guess.

There was silence supreme! Not a shriek, not a scream,
    Scarcely even a howl or a groan,
As the man they called 'Ken' told his story again
    In a gravely oleaginous tone.

'Friends, we're in a fix, and my words I won't mix:
    What the trouble is quite I won't say;
But the Snark's on the loose, and it's learning new tricks
    So we must keep our eyes on the prey.

'If you haven't the stomach to fight, then depart!'
   (They were all of them fond of quotations,
And Henry V did quite well for a start
   Delivered with slick animation):

'For England expects – I forbear to proceed:
   'Tis a maxim tremendous but trite;
This great land of ours will only succeed
   If we win – but are our means right?

I would say to the doubters, Why, Yes, Yes and Yes!
   (What I tell you three times must be true);
If you want to cause maximum Snarkish distress,
   Then just quote from the *Labour Review*.

For a Snark is a timorous kind of a thing –
   You may scare it with Reds or with Greens,
Who will levy new taxes on all those who sing –
   You may paint the most terrifying scenes.

You may bribe it with tax cuts, and musical chairs,
   You may hunt it with glamour and hope;
You may subtly woo it with waterboard shares;
   You may charm it with smiles and soft soap.

You must make sure it's grateful for all its new weath,
   You may flatter its national pride;
But do not refer to the National Health,
   Or mention the pound's on the slide – '

But while he was speaking (flipping back his smooth hair),
   The Bundesbank swiftly drew nigh,
And grabbed Nigel Lawson, who shrieked in despair,
   For he knew that the bank rate was high.

Ken broke off for a moment to stifle a sob,
   Then continued with his peroration,
(Though some heard him mutter, 'Good riddance, the slob!'
   As he bowed to his standing ovation.)

[14 October 1989]

41

Counting Out the Eighties

Oh God, another ten years down the drain;
More damage for the mirror to explain:
Those wisps of gray, new veins across the nose,
The growing paunch that half obscures the toes...

Outside the bathroom door the long-dead news
Is served again in dozens of reviews;
The colour sups dementedly parade
Pictorial pickings from the past decade:

A cast of horribly familiar faces,
The winners of a hundred one-horse races,
The media icons of a ten-year binge
When loads of money was society's hinge –

Money for an image or a slogan;
Money – lots and lots – for Terry Wogan,
And other stars who live the life of Riley:
Madonna, Joan (and Jackie) Collins, Kylie...

Beyond the tabloid visions, wars galore,
Catastrophies, disasters by the score,
Plagues and famines: countless thousands died.
The Third World's poor stayed poor, and multiplied.

But Berlin has outlived its shameful wall,
And last week saw the vile Ceausescus' fall.
As long as Gorbachev still gets his way,
The Stalinists at last have had their day.

While here at home the Liederene ploughs on,
Though many punters think the magic's gone.
The Eighties, clearly, were the Thatcher years,
But Nanny's reign looks set to end in tears.

[30 December 1989]

Curriculum Vitae

Most aspects of life over the last ten years have been affected by Thatcherite values. Education is no exception.

'Pupils face rent bills for School Equipment' – headline

The bike sheds are run by NCP,
   There's a toll at the schoolyard gate.
Forgetting your money is no excuse,
   There's a hefty fine if you're late.

The classrooms are run on a time-share scheme –
   You have to purchase your seat,
And all of your paper and exercise books,
   But they give you a VAT receipt.

Gregory says that he's sub-let his locker;
   Fiona's saved up for PT;
Amanda and Giles have just bought shares
   In Playgrounds Plc.

Kevin and Paul have landed the contract
   Supplying the frogs to the labs.
I've put in for the waste-paper bins,
   And the catering's up for grabs.

Mr MacGregor's curriculum works,
   Why don't you drop in and see,
Just make an appointment – we take all cards –
   And charge a quite reasonable fee.

[27 January 1990]

The Ref Rules, OK?

While defending his world heavyweight title, Mike Tyson was unexpectedly knocked out by the underdog, Buster Douglas. The referee later admitted he'd made a mistake in an earlier count on Douglas, and for a while it looked as though promoter Don King was going to be able to force the boxing authorities to suspend the verdict.

The ref's decision is final,
But which one would you like?
Depends on who you'd like to win,
Buster Douglas – or Mike.

Who'd have thought the business
Of counting up to ten
Could really come to mean so much
To two – very large – grown men?

The punters want excitement,
Everyone wants fair play,
But as any promoter will tell you, son,
The fight game has to pay.

The law of the darkest jungle
Rules outside the ring;
There ain't no lions or tigers there,
But Mr King is king.

By Humpty-Dumpty logic,
Both these men have won:
The world has got two champions;
Either two – or none.

Roll up, roll up for the rematch,
The glad promoters shout:
This is the fight you'll want to see,
So get your cheque-books out.

[17 February 1990]

Holy Willie's Prayer
(after Rabbie Burns)

At the Church of England's General Synod, traditionalists attacked liberal
positions, especially over a recent report on homosexuality within the
Church.

O Lord, in your divine creation
Intercourse for generation
(Well, give or take a calculation)
    Is thy strict law;
Otherwise it's hell's damnation:
      Of that I'm sure.

You gave us naughty parts to tease us,
And willing wives, of course, to please us
When the warm blood's urgings seize us.
    The path is straight
That leads us up to you, Lord Jesus,
      At Heaven's Gate.

I thank thee, Lord, I'm like John Gummer,
Assured through Grace that I'll become a
Halo'ed and Celestial strummer
    In lasting bliss –
Not like the bloke who gives his chum a
      Forbidden kiss.

Love counts for nothing: poofs can't win.
It's only where you put it in
Decides what is or is not sin.
    If you are gay,
Stay celibate or take to gin.
      Now let us pray.

[24 February 1990]

Tried and Tested

More than 17,000 animals are used annually to test cosmetics and toiletries. Companies which refuse to test their products on animals are threatened by a proposed EC directive to impose new, animal-tested safety standards.

It's hard to kick the habit
Of using up a rabbit
To check out the toxicity in things.
But we're happy to comply,
Quite chuffed in fact to die,
To show you if a product kills or stings.

It's jolly being a bunny,
Though your eyes get rather runny
When they drip shampoo into them for a week;
But we feel we've been some use
If a hairspray or a mousse
Gets clearance as being healthy, so to speak.

So shave a patch of skin
And rub the lipstick in;
We'll tell you if it irritates or no.
Oh anything's worthwhile
To enhance a lovely smile
Or add a tincture to your beauty's glow.

Here's to the new directive,
And let's hope it is effective:
Cosmetics must be safe at any price.
They must be tried and tested
(Or you will be arrested)
On beagles, bunnies, guinea-pigs or mice.

[17 March 1990]

48

A Canterbury Tale

With the announcement of Dr Runcie's resignation, Mrs Thatcher had the opportunity to choose a more congenial Archbishop of Canterbury.

Whan that Aprille with opinioun polls
Confirms al Marches plentivous own-goals,
And Kynnock and eek Hattersely look chuffed
For that the Tories in Mid-Staffs ben stuffed;
And Labour activists shout come on sone,
The Wyf of Downing Street hir course hath ronne;
And all the populace is up in armes
Against the tax which hath no winning charmes;
And even somme backbenchers speken rudeliche,
Despite the airs one gives oneself right roialliche;
And Kenneth Clarke, who looketh fat and hale
And hath good cheer for that he loveth ale
Semes likely to mess up the health servyce
Becas he heedeth not doctors' advyce;
And no man spies a way to cut the lede
Which maketh everich Tory herte blede
(Excepting one y-clepped Heseltine,
Who though he much protests, doth not much pine);
And cabinet ben ful of shifty men
Who have their secret hopes of Number Ten;
Then comes a time for leaders' thought to wend
To Caunterbury and ther to pick a frende
In place of Runcie now retyrement's due;
A mighty prelaat of the proper hue,
To give in these dark hours some fleeting hope,
Al dressed fine in mitre bands and cope –
A man of stature and of sound opinioun
In matters both of staat and eek religioun.

[31 March 1990]

Easter Thoughts
(for John Caperon)

We thank thee, Lord, we're happy,
And reasonably well off;
(A shame about the organist's
Irritating cough).

We love the Easter Service,
The whole church looks so bright;
We love all the appointed hymns,
And sing with all our might.

A psalm before the sermon;
How tall the Vicar stands.
It's such a privilege to take
Communion from his hands.

And now we're on our hassocks,
Praying for this and that.
World peace would be a boon (I wish
I'd worn my other hat).

More prayers – for Mrs Thatcher,
The Queen and Terry Waite;
Then fumble through the final hymn
For coins for the plate.

We shuffle to the doorway,
And out into the sun.
I hope I put the oven on;
I hope the lamb is done.

[14 April 1990]

The New Season

Sightscreens, beer tents, empty stands;
    The first few streaky fours;
Fielders blowing on chapped hands;
    Echoey applause.

Bowlers doing a 'little bit';
    A sharp, half-strangled cry:
The batsman gets the benefit,
    And trots an easy bye.

Nervous taps to check the box –
    The bowling looks quite quick;
The bat against the toecap knocks,
    And then a little flick.

A member sets aside his beer
    And cheerfully applauds;
Will this one be the golden year,
    With glory won at Lord's?

Joe Public stolidly unpacks
    His thermos from his bag;
A fiercely gusting wind attacks
    The county's sun-bleached flag.

Four o'clock sees queues for tea,
    Rock cakes and sticky buns;
The diehard faithful hope to see
    A few more hard-earned runs.

A middle order bat departs;
    The sun goes in again.
And so another season starts
    – And stops, of course, for rain.

[21 April 1990]

The Supporter
(after Rupert Brooke)

'We won two world wars and it goes to your head a bit. We are not going to take anything from anybody now. We will just give them a good hiding.' – fan.

As the World Cup approached, a bellicose campaign was promised by a minority of English football supporters.

If I should be arrested, think of me:
    That there's some corner of a foreign town
Which is forever Leeds. United, we
    Got plastered, shouted, fought and then fell down –
Louts whom England bored, made unaware,
    Gave, once, her flowers to trample, streets to roam;
Hooligans of England – shaven hair,
    Tattooed, flag-swathed – at war away from home.

And think, this hero spoiling for a fight,
    And brought up on the wrong side of the fence,
        Gives somewhere back neglect by England given:
Her slights and wounds; dreams brutal as the night;
    A tabloid culture breeding violence
        In hearts by patriotic hatred driven.

[12 May 1990]

One World Down the Drain

One World Week focused on global warming, with a UN report promising
the direst consequences from the greenhouse effect. However, in the clash
between long-term and short-term interests, the future looks likely to be
the loser.

It's goodbye half of Egypt,
    The Maldives take a dive,
And not much more of Bangladesh
    Looks likely to survive.

Europe too will alter,
    Book flights to Venice now.
It won't be there in fifty years –
    Great City. Pity. Ciao.

        But we don't care,
        We won't be there,
            Our acid greenhouse party
        Will carry on
        Until we're gone,
            So bad luck Kiribati

– And all the other atolls
    That sink beneath the seas,
The millions who will suffer from
    Drought, famine and disease.

The weather map is changing
    But what are we to do?
Let's have another conference on
    The ills of CO_2.

        Oh global warming
        's habit-forming,
            But do not rock the boat;
        We're doing our best,
        Although we're pressed
            (The future has no vote).

[26 May 1990]

He Never Expected Much

June 2 was the 150th anniversary of the birth of Thomas Hardy, whose birth-place at Upper Bockhampton, and the landmarks associated with the Wessex novels, have become tourist shrines.

Time's laughing stocks we writers are,
Who hoped our words would travel far,
And move the minds of later folk;
    That's now an idle joke.

Laboriously did we assail
The Mount of Truth: to no avail.
Posterity wants nothing more
    Than souvenirs galore:

Postcards of every private place,
Or T-shirts featuring a face,
Mugs depicting Tess or Jude:
    The madding crowds intrude

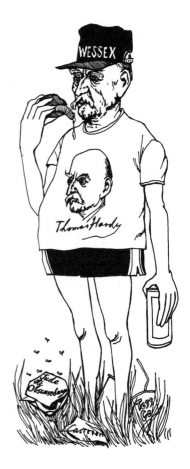

On purlieus sacred once to me
And those I loved a century
Or more ago. What do they seek,
    Peering cheek by cheek?

Ring-pulls now litter Beeny Cliff,
And Castle Boterel is stiff
With coaches, motor-bikes and cars
    And queues for burger bars.

A ring-road circles Casterbridge,
And service stations crown the ridge
That overlooks my Egdon heath.
    I'm glad I lie beneath

The uncommunicative sod,
Where glumly I commune with God
About the mindless rote of Time,
    The emptiness of rhyme.

[2 June 1990]

The Lost Leader
(after Browning)

'Something stops me from saying I shall never rejoin the Labour Party'
– DAVID OWEN.

Just for ambition he took off and left us,
    Just for a party to hold in his sway.
Glamour, high profile, of these he bereft us;
    Limelight at Limehouse was ever his way.
Politics freed from the pressures of faction,
    Civilised values from Shirley and Roy;
Sweetness and light proved a fatal attraction:
    David, the Wonder, was not a nice boy.
Hillhead and Crosby – the new dawn was breaking;
    Power for the pleasant was virtually sure:
PR and *paté de foie* for the taking;
    Fate intervened with a miserable war.
Four became Two and then Two were divided;
    Merger was out in the wake of defeat.
Bunker committees sat down and decided:
    Fight to the end, to the very last seat.
'SDP beaten by Loony in Bootle!'
    Screaming Lord Such was ahead in the poll.
Gone are the glory days: no fifes now tootle,
    Staff will be laid off to sign on the dole.
SDP membership, albeit it dwindling
    Now up for grabs after nearly ten years –
What started handsomely ended in swindling;
    Some party it was, but it ended in tears.
Life's night begins; let him never come back to us!
    There would be doubt, hesitation and pain,
Forced praise on our part – the glimmer of twilight,
    Never glad confident morning again!

[9 June 1990]

Ave Atque Vale: Hail and Farewell, Nicholas Ridley
(AIR: *Deutschland über Alles*)

After a controversial career as one of Mrs Thatcher's right-hand men,
Nicholas Ridley was forced to resign because of unguarded comments in a
Spectator interview about Germany's ambitions to dominate Europe.

Ridley, *Ave atque vale*,
On your bike, in other words.
It was most unwise to sally
Forth on ground that's Douglas Hurd's.
Though the Germans are appalling,
Devious and dark with plots,
(Lebensraum and 'Herr Pohl Calling'),
They're the ones who call the shots.

Wrap the Green Belt tight around you,
Keep the peasants out of sight;
Pray the meadows that surround you
Don't succumb to builders' blight.
Down in Gloucestershire we're certain
Privacy will compensate
For your pulling down the curtain
As a Minister of State.

Having caused a final upset,
Forced at last to step aside,
Off you sail into the sunset
With your bow doors open wide.
Calling Kohl the Great Dictator
Left your colleagues quite aghast.
Now you're simply a *Spectator*,
Stranded on the shelf at last.

[21 July 1990]

Monday, 30 July 1990
In Memoriam Ian Gow MP, murdered by the IRA

The Test match reaching boiling point at Lord's;
    Tailbacks predicted on the motorway;
Along the front, the peeling summer hordes:
    It was a very English sort of day.

Cloud shadows patterning the Sussex Downs,
    The paddocks and pre-harvest fields of wheat;
The traffic threading villages and towns
    Stifled by the tarmac-warping heat.

Another day, with all the diary's plans;
    The postman's knock; the shaving mirror's face.
A boy freewheels along the lane – no hands –
    And someone kneels to tie a trailing lace...

Fast-forward – to the sirens at the gates,
    White tape across the bottom of the drive,
Like those once cut to open stores or fêtes
    In that lost time when he was still alive.

The aftermath usurped by camera crews:
    A hundred talking heads reiterate
That softest targets make the hardest news,
    And that no words can ever compensate.

But still the waves crash on round Beachy Head,
    And seabirds soar and tumble, wheeling free.
A last deckchair is left untenanted,
    Looking obdurately out to sea.

[4 August 1990]

Ozymandias Revisited

Saddam Hussein invaded Kuwait on 2 August 1990.

I met a traveller from a savaged land
Who said: Two lines of tanks rolled into town;
The helpless, headlong corpses strew the sand,
And the survivors suffer that fierce frown,
The thick moustache and sneer of cold command
Which seems to say: 'You might have better read
My passions ere I stamped on you to gain
New oil fields and a coast. Hear overhead
My Mirage fighters grouping, and beware;
My name is President Saddam Hussein:
Look on my arms, ye Mighty, and prepare
To challenge one whose blood-bespattered hands
Hold thousands hostage – that is, if you dare
Risk one colossal wreck athwart the sands.'

[11 August 1990]

58

It's All Over Now

(for Tony Cox)

'Death of the 45' – announced on the *Today* programme, Radio 4.

Bad news this morning buzzed around my ear
Amidst the really serious bad news:
The single's on death row, the end is near
On seven inch, for pop, punk, rock and blues.
    They're killing off the 45 –
    Synonymous with being alive
And young with nothing but your socks to lose.

I tumbled out of bed and dug mine out:
The Stones, Kinks, Beatles, all were there –
She Loves You, It's All Over, Twist and Shout,
And Scott McKenzie, flowers in his hair.
    Bliss was it back in '67
    And to be young was very heaven,
When trousers used to flaunt a Paisley flare.

The wind-up gramophone and 78s
That shattered like clay pigeons – (used to weigh
About the same as china dinner plates) –
Long since have had their dim-remembered day.
    And now the same is true for vinyl:
    The single's doomed; the verdict's final.
Technology has had its brutal way.

Fontana, Decca, Pye and Parlophone...
Their coloured sleeves lie scattered on the floor.
The hours I used to spend upstairs alone
With all my gleanings from the record store –
    Dylan, Jimi Hendrix, Cream –
    Lost in my adolescent dream.
I wish now I had bought a whole lot more.

[25 August 1990]

Gower Power

'When Gower goes out to bat, an entire population usually goes out to bat with him' – Martin Johnson, *The Independent*.

After a disappointing season, Gower reached the Oval Test needing a score to keep his place for the tour of Australia. He responded with his 16th Test century – 157 not out.

My finger hovered, then drew back.
How many times had I switched on
To hear: 'That was a lovely shot:
He's going well – oh...and he's gone'?

I waited until half past twelve.
The picture flickered: he was there.
First shot, a searing cover slash:
One of those days of matchless flair.

A sixteenth century in Tests;
The crowd seemed on the brink of bliss.
Absurd to think of leaving out
A man as talented as this.

The dogs of war are gathering;
Tanks clamber through the desert sand;
A dangerous dictator takes
A child hostage by the hand.

What relevance has sport to life?
You could say, absolutely none.
But what would be the point of it
Without the pleasure and the fun?

And someone doing something well –
Supremely well, in Gower's case –
Gives the average life a lift,
And makes the world a better place.

[1 September 1990]

Timothy Winters 1990
(with apologies to Charles Causley)

'Teacher shortage row marks new school year' – *Guardian* headline.

Timothy Winters comes to school
With about as much chance of winning the pools
As finding a qualified teacher in class
To help with all the exams he must pass.

Some days he's shut out, when no one's there.
Why should Timothy Winters care?
A blitz of a boy, he goes down to the park.
On days like this, school's quite a lark.

Teaching Timothy isn't much fun;
Those who've tried it have often run.
They'll last a week, and then it's Goodbye.
And someone else comes in on supply.

Mr MacGregor dismisses his plight:
'We've 45 ways of putting it right;
We'll advertise widely for new trainees
And make up the short-fall from overseas.

I'm sure we'll be able to make them stay
With regional weighting and flexible pay.
We'll juggle the money and claim there's enough,
And hope the electorate won't call our bluff.'

Mr MacGregor's beginning to glow,
As through his britches the blue winds blow.
Come one Minister, come on ten,
Timothy Winters shouts out: 'When?'

[8 September 1990]

Hymn: No Turning Back
(TUNE: *'Lift up your Hearts!' We lift them, Lord to thee*)

The right-wing No Turning Back group published a pamphlet indicating their hopes for a fourth term under Mrs Thtcher. It included proposals for compulsory private health insurance for all, and community work for those unwilling or unable to pay.

No turning back! We've only just begun!
We can't stop now, the job is but half done!
No turning back! There's so much more to do,
And our Great Leader's pledged to see it through.

When every one is on insurance schemes,
We'll have the health service of all our dreams.
We can't protect the feckless or the weak;
But it's not them to whom we wish to speak.

Dependency has long become a drug;
From under scroungers we will pull the rug.
The poor will pay, or failing that they'll work;
There will not be a chance for them to shirk.

Below the level of all former years
Expenditure will shrink to cut arrears.
No turning back! Reforms are here to stay:
The Welfare State must this time pass away.

So faithful souls, who recognise what's right,
Come raise your cheque-books for the fateful fight.
No turning back! We're promised to the cause.
It's conference time; let's hear the loud applause.

Then as the trumpet call rings in our ears,
Announcing that we've won yet five more years,
Still shall those hearts respond with full accord,
And Tory stalwarts reap their just reward.

[22 September 1990]

Pol Pot: The Second Coming

In a television programme, *Cambodia: The Betrayal* (ITV) and a long
article in the *Weekend Guardian*, John Pilger again exposed the United
States' clandestine support for Pol Pot and the Khmer Rouge, and the
British Government's complicity in the policy.

As the great roots crush the Ankor Wat
The stones and lintels of a nation split,
Prised apart by a nightmare. This is it:
A tiger crouching back towards Year Dot.
(The tiger is so fierce it can't be tamed.)

Can we believe it? We've seen it once before:
The wind blowing through whitening bones,
And History's age-old stepping stones,
The fresh skulls bedded in the jungle floor?
(The horror is so great it can't be named.)

The faces stare impassively out at us,
All found guilty of the usual crime:
Born in the wrong place, at the wrong time;
Faraway people, they died with little fuss.
(Brown Belsens far away – we can't be blamed.)

Pol Pot's shy smile, and 'Genocide'
Diminishes to 'Human rights abuses'.
Language has its uses
To salve a powerful nation's injured pride.
(There's no such policy – or so it's claimed.)

To salve a powerful nation's injured pride,
To gain revenge upon the Vietnamese,
The children's legs are blown off at the knees,
With 'mines technology' that we've supplied.
(Our taxes pay for children to be maimed.)

In grand hotels the diplomats convene;
They've so much to discuss over their lunch:
The final form of words, the crunch.
Their consciences, like serviettes, are clean.
(These people can't, apparently, be shamed.)

[13 October 1990]

Lester Rides Again

'This is the most brilliant, abiding genius that any century will ever see'
– Brough Scott in the *Independent on Sunday*. 'You have one leg each side
of the horse' – Lester Piggott when asked if he had changed his riding tech-
nique after his enforced absence from the race-track.

Gee-up Lester Piggott,
    The divots punch the sky,
One for the happy punter,
    One in the tax-man's eye.

Gee-up Lester Piggott,
    With a leg on either side,
Your technique hasn't changed much.
    You simply ride and ride.

A legend in your lifetime
    For judgment, verve and speed,
On a grey day in mid-October
    A winner's what we need.

The odds are getting shorter.
    A fiver says you'll win.
The Tote queue's half-way round the tent;
    The tic-tac man's done in.

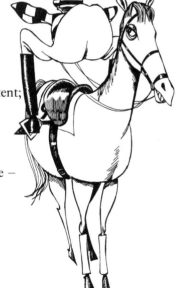

They're under starter's orders,
    A kerfuffle at the start:
Then arse in the air and head for home –
    You really look the part.

Thank you, Lester Piggott,
    You've made the afternoon –
Back in the winner's enclosure
    Not a single minute too soon.

[20 October 1990]

Ode to Autumn

In a party political broadcast on the eve of the Eastbourne by-election
(which the Conservatives lost to the Liberal Democrats), Kenneth Baker
was keen to enlist John Keats as a Tory, adapting the famous opening line
of *Ode to Autumn* to disparage the 'mists' of the Labour conference at
Blackpool and commend the 'fruitfulness' of the Conservative conference
at Bournemouth.

Spokesman of myths and mellow fruitiness,
    Close bosom friend to the maturing One;
Conspiring with her how to load and bless
    The Thatcher years with yet another run;
To bend the voters' ears with pleasantries,
        Purveyed in oratory that's over-ripe;
            To swell each word, and plump each pregnant phrase,
        To propagate your propaganda's tripe.
The party faithful hum and buzz like bees,
Some think the rapt applause will never cease,
        As you continue ladling out the praise.

Where are the vaunts of conference? Where are they?
    Think not of them, or it will make you blue, –
As brightly plumaged birds enjoy their day
    And tinge sour grapes with such a ghastly hue.
Now in a wailful choir the agents mourn,
    Along the pier, along the promenade;
        Excuses will not do, not do at all;
It was no fluke that cost you 'safe' Eastbourne;
    Although you will continue smiling hard,
    It's no use claiming fealty from the bard:
        For after Autumn comes Hyperion's Fall.

[27 October 1990]

Rae's Elegy on a Leadership Challenge

Sir Geoffrey Howe's resignation engendered intense speculation that there would be a challenge to Mrs Thatcher in November 1990, either from a stalking horse, or a heavyweight candidate like Michael Heseltine.

The curfew tolls the knell of parting day,
And Douglas Hurd winds slowly home to tea.
A stalking horse, if one were found, would say:
'I do this for my party, not for me.'

But Mrs Thatcher sits in Number Ten,
Preparing, should she need her own campaign,
To crush those few, who, trespassing again,
Molest her ancient solitary reign.

For she's ordained to rule, and rule alone,
'Tis folly to suppose she could resign, –
Surrender voluntarily her throne,
And leave the world to Michael Heseltine.

And once the challenger's declared, no power
In Westminster or on the Earth can save
The victim from th'inevitable hour.
The quest for glory leads but to the grave.

The knife will slip between the shoulder-blades.
The graveyard heaves with many a mouldering heap
Where, impotent and once-familiar shades,
The sacked Forefathers of the rebels sleep.

For them no more the blazing public row,
The busy Premier plying her searing scorn.
Far from the madding crowd Sir Geoffrey Howe
Enjoys retirement's incense-breathing Morn.

[10 November 1990]

End of the Road

Finally it happened. After eleven years in power, Mrs Thatcher resigned. She withdrew from the leadership race before the second ballot, having declared that she would fight on regardless. The announcement was as sudden as it was unexpected. The following was rushed out as a replacement for the original poem in the two or three hours remaining before the page's deadline.

She's gone. The quite unthinkable
Has actually at last occurred.
Fight on! Fight on! But fight on, Major,
Fight on, Hurd.

She's gone, the towering figure's toppled,
Pole-axed by her own poll tax,
And several rather nicely judged
Backbench attacks.

Eleven years the nation banged
Its head against a solid wall.
Today the edifice has gone
For good and all.

Crowds gather on the promontory;
The Iron Lady's towed away.
The hastily convened violins
Begin to play.

[24 November 1990]

Drinking Song for Christmas

The annual anti drink-driving campaign was led by a very 'strong' TV advert-
isement, featuring a family torn apart by the father's killing of a child while
over the legal limit. But according to a Guardian report, 'a hard core of
offenders between 35 and 50 will drink on regardless of the consequences'.

Same old friendly faces
    Lined up along the bar.
I don't mind if I do, old chap.
    No, I'm not driving far,
And no one stops a businessman
    Safe in his smart car.

It takes just one tight corner;
    One tight driver's all it takes:
Hands pale against the headlights,
    A futile squeal of breaks –
And several lifetimes living,
    Living with your mistakes.

Hands are shaking badly,
    Must be shock, or fear.
No movement under the blanket.
    I'd rather not go near.
I'll gladly make a statement,
    Of course. What, blow in here?

Don't like that face in the mirror,
    Don't like that face at all.
Can't meet the eyes of my children;
    They make me feel so small.
An extra hour in the local
    Came before my fall.

[8 December 1990]

Enjoying the Festive Season

Research shows that the Christmas holiday period is a time of stress.

The week between two booze-ups
Is the low point of the year.
We sit at home and watch the box
And drink our cans of beer,

Putting off those letters
Beginning, 'Thank you for –'
A lot of things we didn't want,
Or got the year before.

We're fed up with the turkey;
We're fed up with the gales.
The mood we're in we might as well
Boycott the bloody sales.

Half the children's presents
Have now gone on the blink.
A dozen TV dinners sit
Abandoned in the sink.

Drag out the Fitness Manual
And think about a jog.
Well, maybe once around the park
To exercise the dog.

If I see one more Turtle
I'll roast it in its skin.
When can I go back to work?
And when does term begin?

[29 December 1990]

Soft Targets

Shortly after the expiry of the UN deadline for Iraq to withdraw from Kuwait, the war began, with massive Allied bombing of strategic targets in Iraq. Hostilities broke out in the middle of school exams in Iraqi schools.

The church clock strikes the hour: it's 12 o'clock.
Gloved and scarved against the chill
The pigeon lady comes to feed her flock.
The crusts spill out, and down the pigeons spill.
I sip my second coffee and take stock.
A cyclist changes gear to take the hill.

My neighbour comes back with her shopping done.
A girl is waiting for a bus.
A jogger is enjoying his lunchtime run.
A couple take a stroll. They could be us,
Chatting as they walk, enjoying the sun.
The day's developing its impetus.

The bus has come: the girl has disappeared.
Some laughing schoolgirls cross the road.
They're full of fun, however carefully reared.
A carrier staggers underneath his load.
A carpet seller with a grizzled beard
Tots up the sums of money he is owed.

Sandals, slippers, scuff the sandy street
As people take the evening air.
This group are friends who regularly meet
To drink sweet tea together in the square,
Recuperating from the sapping heat.
And then the muezzin calls for evening prayer.

[19 January 1991]

White Hats, Black Hats

General Schwarzkopf, the Commander of Allied forces in the Gulf likened
the war to a Western, with the Coalition forces the good guys in white hats
ranged against baddies in black hats. It remained one of the war's ironies
that the West had been largely responsible for supplying Saddam Hussein's
vast arsenal, and, in the case of Britain, for advising on the construction
of bunkers which sheltered Iraq's airforce from Allied attacks.

In war our guys are white as snow,
    The baddies, oil-slick black.
The monster with the big moustache
    Gets all the moral flak.

But things are otherwise in peace;
    It doesn't work like that.
Money's far more vital than
    The colour of the hat.

We have to weigh our interests up.
    Morality is grey.
Tomorrow's evil enemy
    May be a friend today.

We'll overlook his vicious side,
    That massacre of Kurds,
(Conventions guarding human rights
    Are merely forms of words),

And greet him with a chummy smile,
    And shake him by the hand,
And build him bomb-proof bunkers deep
    Beneath the desert sand.

But don't those million dollar sales,
    Those contracts in the sun,
Seem rather poor investments now
    The shooting has begun?

Our smiling erstwhile customer
    Is now the Prince of Lies,
Committing vile atrocities,
    Surprise, surprise, surprise...

[2 February 1991]

Equations

'Hospital refuses to pay for patient's treatment' – *Independent* headline.
'3 Tank Shells Equal One Human Life' – *Mirror* headline.
'Taking life is a very expensive business now' – *Mirror* quote.

Yes, clinical destruction
Can cost an arm and leg:
The Chancellor has made his rounds
To browbeat and to beg,

And all our helpful allies
Have coughed up what they can.
Someone always foots the bill
When man is killing man.

In fact, the sky's the limit
(From which a fortune falls –
Equivalent each week of war
To several hospitals).

Yet when it comes to health care
The costs must be contained:
'We've overspent on drugs this year,'
the hospital explained.

'And so, we're very sorry,
There's nothing more to do:
Goodbye, God bless, take care, good luck
(And that's an end of you).'

Life and death decisions
Are hard enough to make;
And still the war costs rise and rise
With every life we take.

[9 February 1991]

Cockroach Chorus
(with apologies to Louis MacNeice)

A very graphic Channel 4 documentary exposed the current plague of cockroaches in inner-city tower blocks.

John MacDonald found a roach hiding under the sofa,
Waited till it came to light and hit it with a poker.
Annie MacDougal making tea saw one pop from the toaster;
It scuttled into the children's room and underneath a poster.

It's no go the spray-guns, it's no go the Harpic,
The bleeders run all over the place and go to ground in the carpet.

They keep the kids awake at night and crawl all over the baby;
Ring the council to ask for help, a voice on the phone says 'Maybe'.
Mrs Carmichael killed her fifth, looked at the job with revulsion,
Said to the man from Pest Control, 'They're spread like lumpy
        emulsion.'

It's no go the football pools, it's no go the horses,
All we want is a decent flat, or a council with proper resources.

It's no go the government grants, it's no go the election,
Sit on your arse for half your life waiting for an inspection.
It's no go the tax relief if you haven't got a mortgage,
All we want is a lump sum as deposit with the Norwich.

It's no go insecticide with a mask against pollution;
Get the men back time again, and still there's no solution.
One jumped into the baby's milk just as it was warming.
Squash the bastards under your heel, there'll still be more in
        the morning.

[23 March 1991]

COCKROACH
CHORUS

Son of Poll Tax
(Anyone Can Play)

In the aftermath of the promised abolition of the Poll Tax, Nigel Lawson coined the expression 'Son of Poll Tax'. Speculation as to the replacement local government tax ran riot.

A new tax – a view tax?
A Not-Me-But-You tax?
A blue tax? a loo tax?
A Tories-In-A-Stew tax?

A roof tax? A hoof tax?
A rather more aloof tax?
A spoof tax? A pouffe?
A Let-Me-See-The-Proof tax?

A theme tax? A beam tax?
A Not-what-it-might-seem tax?
A dream tax? A scream tax?
A printout-by-the-ream tax?

A lane tax? A vane tax?
A money-down-the-drain tax?
A brain tax? A mane tax?
A Here-we-go-again tax?

A key tax? A knee tax?
A You-but-oh-not-Me tax?
A flea tax? A tea tax?
A Glad-we-all-agree tax?

A late tax? A wait tax?
A This-is-not-a-rate tax?
A fête tax? A gate tax?
A Let's-have-more-debate tax?

A Mum tax? A dumb tax?
A High-street-down-to-slum tax?
A thumb tax? A bum tax?
A Tweedledee-and-Dum tax?

A troll tax? A prole tax?
A slightly-less-own-goal tax?
A shoal tax? A sole tax?
– An Anything-but-Poll Tax!

[30 March 1991]

Memo

When the Kurdish rebellion, largely inspired by broad hints of support from
President Bush, failed, and Saddam Hussein resorted to the same brutal
repression that he had constantly used in the past, the Allies stood back,
claiming it was none of their business and that the terms of the ceasefire
agreement prevented any intervention. As the Kurds fled to the mountains,
Douglas Hurd the Foreign Secretary, flew to Beijing for top level talks with
the same Chinese leadership that had ordered the massacre in Tiananmen
Square in June 1989.

We have no mandate to assist
A rebel army to resist
Terror on whatever scale,
Nor to shield you if you fail.
You claim we promised you our aid?
That is an error I'm afraid –
Just one of George's little slips;
Read the small print, not his lips.

We could have done it in the war.
You should have struck some weeks before
When everything was black and white.
But now to help you in your fight
Would not be quite 'appropriate'.
Kuwait was, after all, Kuwait,
And no one should confuse repression
With international aggression.

Saddam Hussein is back on side –
Which leaves him free for genocide.
Well, everybody makes mistakes,
And rehabilitation takes
On average just about two years,
Provided no more Tiananmen Squares
Or other unbecoming scenes
Appear upon our TV screens.

We're working for the New World Order.
It hasn't reached the Turkish border
Or the Middle East quite yet,
But that's a hiccup we'll forget –
A little Easter rinse of hands –
Everybody understands
Just what we can and cannot do
For stateless refugees like you.

[6 April 1991]

Go Tell It On The Mountain

It was greatly to John Major's credit that he responded so swiftly and deter-
minedly to the huge public pressure that built up over the Kurdish issue,
and after lagging behind other nations like France and Italy, Britain led the
way over safe havens for the Kurds. In the first week, however, there was
much uncertainty as to exactly what – or where – these enclaves might be.

Go tell it on the mountain,
The enclave is at hand.
It has no weak foundation
In mud or soil or sand.

It has no earthly borders,
It isn't on the map,
But it will keep the people
Safe from Saddam's trap.

Go tell it on the mountain,
Where still the thousands die,
Huddled under plastic sheets
Beneath a hostile sky.

Go tell it to the soldiers
Who drove us from the plain,
Go tell it to the border guards
Who drive us back again.

Our towns have all been shattered,
Our villages are razed,
But we'll have walls of canvas,
So let the powers be praised.

Go tell it on the mountain,
The new safe haven's here –
Well, if not here exactly,
Then somewhere very near.

Go tell it on the mountain,
Salvation has arrived,
Or will have any minute now –
For those who have survived.

Go tell it on the mountain
Where still the people die,
Eating snow for water
Beneath a hostile sky.   [13 April 1991]

Sonnet: The Bard's Complaint

Just as Prince Charles came out with criticism that Shakespeare wasn't being taught properly in our schools, it was announced that after twenty years the Bard was to be replaced on the £20 note by Sir Michael Faraday (1791-1867), who discovered electrical induction and the laws of electromagnetism. The Bank of England said that Shakespeare had 'had a long innings and we felt that his time had come'.

O from what power hast thou this powerful might,
To push my visage from its wonted place,
Making my bright day the darkest night?
And who will recognise your obscure face?
Electro-magnetism makes you shine,
But quote me one thing that you said or wrote
That people can remember – just a line
That warrants your appearance on *my* note.
You can't, of course you can't. It's true that time
Hath at his back a wallet or a purse
For has-beens, but I really thought my rhyme
Would save me from oblivion – or worse.
    There is more brilliance in my slightest play
    Than in a myriad light-bulbs, Faraday.

[20 April 1991]

A Supplicant's Swan Song
(with apologies to Betjeman)

Shortly after Mr Major was allowed to jump the queue for membership of the MCC, an attempt to change the rules to allow the application of Rachel Heyhoe-Flint, former captain of the England women's team, was rejected in a vote by the 17,000 male members.

Ms R. Heyhoe-Flint, Ms R. Heyhoe-Flint,
Applications like yours can cause members to squint.
The Long Room – with women in? – you've got a nerve:
Lord's is the chauvinist's last male preserve.

A classical batsman, your leg-glance a joy,
A Captain of England – but never a boy.
And that is your failing, that is what shocks –
You never, but never, had need of a box.

Miss Joan Hunter Dunn, Miss Joan Hunter Dunn
Got knocked out of Wimbledon – she never won.
But everyone said, 'Oh what bad luck – she tried!'
Her entrée to tennis clubs was never denied.

John Major, though promising, wasn't that great
But suddenly no one saw his need to wait.
A 9,000 waiting list – he bypassed the queue.
They wouldn't, alas, do the same thing for you.

Ms R. Heyhoe-Flint, Ms R. Heyhoe-Flint,
I wonder, oh won't you just give us a hint
As to why you should want to join in down at Lord's
With the rhubarb and custard, and purple-faced hordes,

Amidst stale pints of bitter and quadruple Bells
And those leathery, pipe-smokey, ever-male smells?
What is the attraction – to snooze in the sun
And know you are safe from Miss Joan Hunter Dunn?

[4 May 1991]

Holy Willie's Hellfire Sermon
(with apologies to Burns, again)

'Good and evil. Heaven and hell. You can't have one without the other'
– Peter Mullin in a *Face to Faith* article attacking the Archbishop of York
for discounting the existence of hell (*Guardian*, 10 June 1991).

No sinner is beyond God's reach,
Divine revenge is what we preach
(It's what our Saviour used to teach):
    The one Creator
Will take his fury out on each
    Sly masturbator.

The slaves of promiscuity –
And all who dare to disagree
With our self-righteous ministry –
    In hell's rank stew
Will surely boil. It won't be me
    But might be you –

Along with babies unbaptised,
The unshorn and the circumcised
Of other faiths – they're stigmatised.
    Yes, all must bubble
In torture landscapes fantasised
    By Bosch and Brueghel.

Archbishop Hapgood is an ass,
Dismissing punishment as crass,
Discounting as a sado-mas-
    ochistic farce
Dire hell's necessity. Alas,
    All sinners pass

Before that awful Judgement Seat.
God's omniscience is complete;
There is no point in being discreet,
    For He sees all.
Beneath each surreptitious sheet
    His gaze will fall.

Divinely ordered retribution –
Hell as Heaven's institution –
Is our religious contribution
    To moral conscience.
Liberalism's a pollution,
    Abhorrent nonsense!

No bleeding heart's modernity
Can shake hellfire's fraternity.
As proof of God's paternity
    We all applaud
His Auschwitz for eternity.
    O praise the Lord!

[15 June 1991]

Ballad: The Grocer and the Grocer's Daughter

Ted Heath, when Prime Minister, was nicknamed The Grocer. Mrs Thatcher
was a grocer's daughter.

The Grocer and the Grocer's Daughter
   Were shipwrecked on the shore;
Together they tried hard to think
   What lives they lived before.

'I think I ruled a great country,
   I was, I'm sure, its queen,
And did the most tremendous things
   That anyone had seen.'

'No, no!' the Grocer said, 'it was
   A paltry nation state;
You threw its destiny away:
   You would not integrate.'

The Grocer's Daughter then replied
   With haughty majesty:
'Your reign was short, and many thought
   That you failed abjectly.'

The Grocer looked at her aghast:
   'All right, then we'll dispute
Each policy that you put forth –
   Your brain is quite minute.

Your legacy is ruinous,
   The things you did were wrong;
I reached my peak, my Three-Day-Week
   Showed Britain I was strong.'

'No, Mr Grocer, that won't do –
   You mustn't go so fast.
How long – if you can now recall –
   Exactly did you last?'

A doctor then along the strand
   Just happened to pass by.
He waved his stethoscope aloft
   And then he gave a sigh:

'A case like this is terminal
    I'll confidently state.
The symptoms are extremely clear:
    Unbridled mutual hate.

There is no cure, along this shore
    For those whom time forgot.'
Just then he heard a distant cry
    And more than just one shot.

A half-pay Major struggled there
    The blood poured from his jaw.
With heavy panting breath he cried:
    'This isn't peace it's war.

They are assassins both of them,
    Despite their solemn vow
To stand by me, and the EC,
    Look what they've cocked up now.'

He struggled manfully to rise
    But just as often slipped.
Around his neck, he wore the wreck
    Of what was once his ship.

He had been shot through both his feet,
    And also through his heart.
The guilty parties stood aside,
    They also stood apart.

They had to stand apart you see
    To serve the cause of rhyme.
And while apart they muttered thus:
    'That was a dreadful crime.'

Although they both of them agreed
    It was a frightful shame
Each one protested innocence:
    The other was to blame.

The doctor cracked his knuckle-bones,
    And smoothed his hair in glee:
'This reminds me of the case
    Of my own SDP.

Allow me to pull on my gloves
    Of finest rubber made...'
Around his thin and bloodless lips
    A fearsome smile it played.

'No no!' the Major shrieked in fear,
    'I know that dreadful smile.'
'There is no help along the beach,
    No, not for many a mile.'

The Doctor sadly shook his head,
    And then he rubbed his hands.
The Major lay there at his feet,
    His lifeblood stained the sands.

And as he sighed his latest sigh
    And breathed his latest breath
The Doctor stroked his chin and mused
    On politics and death.

'How truly, truly strange it seems
    It should be always me
That's present at the deathbed scene.
    It must be destiny...'

Meanwhile the two antagonists
    Continued with their fight
And raved and ranted as they walked
    Towards the coming night.

The idle waves washed up the beach
    And then they did withdraw;
The footsteps that were printed there
    Were visible no more.

[22 June 1991]

Executive
(after Betjeman)

Salary increases in excess of 50% for executives in the newly privatised industries have been causing the government embarrassment. When asked at Prime Minister's Question Time if he agreed they were too high, Mr Major said simply, 'Yes sir!'

I am a chief executive, no pay than mine is higher;
My salary's exorbitant. I am a smart high-flyer.
At Question Time a question on the question of my rise
Brought forth from the Prime Minister the tersest of replies.

But though he may be furious, he's impotent to act.
The market sets my salary and that, sir, is a fact,
And every single member of my very loyal board
Agrees with me that I should reap a full and fair reward.

Lots of poor executives are queuing for the dole.
Security is based upon monopoly control.
What you want's an industry supplying a basic need –
You then command a salary that's tailored to your greed.

Executives like me are paid n thousand pounds a week.
You could, if you'd a mind to, cost each single word I speak –
And really it's a snip because we're very decent chaps –
And we have got our fingers on your sockets, phones and taps.

[29 June 1991]

Finale
(for Richard Boston)

While Viv Richards was making his last Test appearance at the Oval, the
completely unknown John Daley was powering his way to the US PGA
Championship, having driven for seven hours when phoned at the last
minute to make up the numbers.

It starts as always with some unknown
Chucking his kit in the booℒ of the car,
And beginning a journey that ends some twenty years on
In the adulation of an ageing superstar.

Ansafones left on all over the city,
Secretaries primed with 'He's at an important meeting'.
Pinstripes and T-shirts jostling to fill
The last available public seating

And the bug eyes of a hundred binoculars
Trained from the anonymous shadow of the stands
On the casual unmistakable figure at slip
With the boxer's shoulders and stone mason's hands,

As the runs whittled down to the grand improbable finale
Of an afternoon no one present will ever forget –
Nor remember, for all England's gratifying glory,
Without a lingering twinge of regret.

[17 August 1991]

92

History Calls in August

One Monday morning in August 1991 the world was shocked by the news of putsch in Russia, replacing President Gorbachev with a committee of hardliners. Resistance to the coup, focused on the heroic figure of Boris Yeltsin, was successful in the end, but it seemed touch and go at the time.

It looked like being an uneventful week.
Then something happened: History made a call.
He didn't knock. He didn't wipe his feet,
But hung his hat up in the hall.

'I get so bored in August,' he complained:
'The whole world stops to get an effing tan.'
But summer's nice and peaceful, I replied.
'Peace! With my attention span?

Economic progress, social trends,
The role of women, health and education!
Don't make me laugh! What history's about
Is simple: bloody confrontation.

Coups and counter-coups, the barricades,
Bloodshed on the streets, the steady roar
Of battle like a tidal wave approaching;
That's what history's really for.

Late summer brings the roll of tanks – and heads;
The rat-tat-tat of gunfire in the night,
Encircling troops drawn up in faceless ranks,
Whole populations put to flight.'

He gave a laugh: 'I hope you like the show.'
And then he left. He didn't shut the door.
He may be back. He didn't say. We all
Remember what he did before.

[24 August 1991]

Toppled

'Drink and lies fuelled coup; the putsch failed through farce and incompetence.' – *Guardian* headline. The coup failed. Boris Yeltsin and the reformers were vindicated, and the old regime finally gave up the ghost. Huge crowds gathered to cheer the removal of statues.

The statues in the end were hollow;
Lenin's down; the rest must follow:
The domineering old erections
Toppled and removed in sections.

Admonitory fingers wag
As cast-iron knees begin to sag;
The noble beards, heroic hair,
Float suspended in mid-air.

And so the evil empire's ended,
The tyranny that cant befriended;
The great inversions: *Pravda* – lies;
Fraternity, mere swatting flies;

Freedom, miles of barbarous wire
And gaoler armies primed to fire;
The Gulag disciplined by ice,
Starvation, torture, fear and lice;

Equality ensured the right
To queue for food for half the night,
While every petty commissar
Gorged happily on caviar.

But apparatchiks on the make
Have made their final big mistake:
Plotters more than three-parts pissed
Aimed for the sun and stars and missed.

Without the secateurs of terror
To prune the tentacles of error,
Privilege, corruption, greed
Eventually ran to seed.

[31 August 1991]

Postcard, Radio

After 1763 days, Terry Waite was finally released. His first contact with the outside world, after four years, was a postcard of a stained glass window showing John Bunyan in Bedford jail. Some time after that he was given a radio on which he listened to the BBC World Service.

No sun, no stars, no wind, no rain;
Life measured by a callous chain;
No air to breathe, no space, no light,
No dawn, no dusk, no day, just night;

The world outside mere noises off:
A clapped-out engine's distant cough,
Gunfire, shouting in the street,
A nagging narrative of feet...

No exercise, no room to move,
The days set in a rigid groove;
No friendly face, no friendly voice;
No decisions, and no choice.

No books, no paper, pencil, pen,
No contact with the world of men,
No post, no fax, no telephone:
Alone, alone, and still alone

For days and weeks and months and years,
A life bricked in by its arrears.
What chronicles of wasted time,
Betrayal of an active prime.

And then one day the bearded guard
Brought in an unexpected card:
Which showed a man inside his cell
(Doing – with paper, ink – quite well),

Another stubborn man of God,
A natural for the Awkward Squad –
And through the bars a hand stretched out
Reproving boredom, grief and doubt.

And then they brought the radio:
And everybody said Hello,
A Tower of Babel breaking in –
The world's companionable din...

[23 November 1991]